WITNESS
TO REVOLUTION, WAR, AND VICTORY

STUDY GUIDE

Over 250 Guided Reading Questions

A Timeline of the American Revolution

Useful Primary Sources

Lists of Important People, Events, and Places of the Revolution

MICHAEL CECERE

Heritage Books
2026

HERITAGE BOOKS
AN IMPRINT OF HERITAGE BOOKS, INC.

Books, CDs, and more—Worldwide

For our listing of thousands of titles see our website
at
www.HeritageBooks.com

Published 2026 by
HERITAGE BOOKS, INC.
Publishing Division
5810 Ruatan Street
Berwyn Heights, MD 20740

Heritage Books by the author:

A Brave, Active, and Intrepid Soldier: Lieutenant Colonel Richard Campbell of the Virginia Continental Line
A Good and Valuable Officer: Daniel Morgan in the Revolutionary War
A Universal Appearance of War: The Revolutionary War in Virginia, 1775–1781
An Officer of Very Extraordinary Merit: Charles Porterfield and the American War for Independence, 1775–1780
Captain Thomas Posey and the 7th Virginia Regiment
Cast Off the British Yoke: The Old Dominion and American Independence, 1763–1776
Great Things are Expected from the Virginians: Virginia in the American Revolution
He Fell a Cheerful Sacrifice to His Country's Glorious Cause: General William Woodford of Virginia, Revolutionary War Patriot
In This Time of Extreme Danger: Northern Virginia in the American Revolution
Second to No Man but the Commander in Chief: Hugh Mercer, American Patriot
They Are Indeed a Very Useful Corps: American Riflemen in the Revolutionary War
They Behaved Like Soldiers: Captain John Chilton and the Third Virginia Regiment, 1775–1778
To Hazard Our Own Security: Maine's Role in the American Revolution
Virginia's Continentals, 1775–1778: Volume One
Virginia's Continentals, 1778–1783: Volume Two
Wedded to My Sword: The Revolutionary War Service of Light Horse Harry Lee
Williamsburg at War: Virginia's Colonial Capital in the Revolutionary War
Witness to Revolution: Growing Up in Williamsburg During the American Revolution
Michael and Jennifer Cecere
Witness to War: The Sequel to Witness to Revolution: Growing Up in Williamsburg During the American Revolution
Michael and Jennifer Cecere
Witness to Victory: The Final Book of Witness to Revolution
Michael and Jennifer Cecere
Witness to Revolution, War, and Victory Study Guide

International Standard Book Number
Paperbound: 978-0-7884-4967-3

Table of Contents

Historical Background

Virginia Before the Revolution

The English colony of Virginia was already 150 years old when the **French and Indian War,** an important event that led to the **American Revolution**, occurred. First established as **Jamestown** in 1607, Virginia's early settlers fought with the native **Powhatan** for several decades to gain control of the land along the James and York Rivers. Both groups endured great hardship in this conflict.

The introduction of South American **tobacco** to Virginia in 1616 by **John Rolfe** provided the English colonists with a valuable **cash crop.** The money earned from tobacco encouraged a steady flow of European settlers to Virginia. As a result, the colony's population and settlements steadily expanded. By the mid-1600's, the English had firm control of the **Tidewater region** of Virginia.

The high demand for tobacco in Europe encouraged Virginians to plant as much as possible. Clearing new land and tending the tobacco plants was very hard. Thousands of poor English and Europeans were willing to come to Virginia to grow tobacco, but they had little money to pay for the voyage. The solution was **indentured servitude**. A colonist in need of more workers for their tobacco fields, or servants for their home, would pay for the cost of someone's trip across the ocean. In return, the new, indebted arrival would sign a contract agreeing to work for the colonist for a certain number of years until their debt was paid off. The length of service was usually four to seven years long, during which the **indentured servant** had little freedom and was often treated harshly.

Once their time of service was over and their debt was paid, indentured servants were released from their servitude and free to do as they please in Virginia. This usually meant becoming tobacco farmers themselves on land that they rented or eventually bought.

Although thousands of indentured servants came to the American colonies every year, there was still a need for more labor to grow more tobacco. As a result, by 1660, more and more Virginians turned to a new source of labor, **slavery**.

Thousands of **enslaved Africans** were brought to Virginia prior to the American Revolution. Most grew tobacco and other crops just like indentured servants. Others worked as household servants or learned specific trades like blacksmithing and carpentry. One big difference between slavery and indentured servitude was that enslaved people were viewed as property or possessions under the law and kept enslaved for their entire lives. And when they had children, the children became slaves too. By the eve of the Revolutionary War, **four out of ten people in Virginia were enslaved Africans**. Just over half of the two thousand inhabitants of Virginia's capital, Williamsburg, were enslaved.

Virginia was not the only British colony in North America. By 1770, fourteen British colonies stretched along the North American coastline from Maine to Florida. Britain also gained control of Quebec and Nova Scotia (Canada) as a result of its victory over the French in the French and Indian War. Of all these colonies, Virginia had the largest population and was the most prosperous, which made it very important to the **British empire**.

Great Britain benefitted from the valuable **natural resources** of its American colonies, particularly the cash crops of tobacco and **sugar cane** (produced in the British Caribbean colonies). A series of British laws called the **Navigation Acts** controlled the trade of the colonies, who in turn, received protection from the British navy and army. Britain's leaders, distracted by important events in Britain and Europe for much of the 1600's and early 1700's, allowed the colonies in America to largely govern themselves with **colonial legislatures** (Assemblies) and **royal governors** (appointed by the King). This system worked well for over 150 years and most colonists in British America were proud to be part of the British empire. They felt both prosperous and free.

Road to Revolution

The French and Indian War, however, which lasted nearly a decade (from 1754-1763), left the British government with an **enormous debt**. Although the American colonies had contributed both soldiers and money to the war, the British parliament believed the colonists should pay more in the form of new taxes to help pay down the debt.

In 1765, the British parliament passed a **Stamp Tax** upon the colonists. This was a tax upon all paper items in the colonies. Marriage licenses, deeds, newspapers, writing paper and even playing cards were just some of the items that the tax applied to.

Most colonists immediately objected, claiming that the British parliament, elected by voters in Great Britain (not the colonies), had no right to impose a tax to raise **revenue** (money) upon the colonists. The argued that the members of Parliament represented the people of England, not the colonists in America. Opponents to the Stamp Tax adopted the slogan "**No Taxation Without Representation**," and many called for a **boycott** of the taxed paper goods. If colonists stopped buying the taxed items, the British government could not earn any revenue from them.

Other colonists went further and attacked British officials. Some were **tarred and feathered** while others had their homes vandalized by mobs. Some in Parliament also objected to the Stamp Tax as an **unconstitutional** law. They agreed with the colonists that Parliament had no right to levy a tax directly upon the colonists in order to raise revenue (collect money) because the colonists did not vote in parliamentary elections. They agreed with the view of "no taxation without representation". The only taxes Parliament was allowed to levy on the colonists, argued supporters in Britain who agreed with the colonists, were **tariffs** on imported goods from other countries.

The unrest in the American colonies caused by the Stamp Act and the arguments against the unconstitutional law by some members of Parliament caused British leaders to **repeal** the law just a year later. This pleased the colonists in America greatly, but there was a catch. Parliament wanted to make sure the colonists understood and accepted that it had the right to, "**govern the colonies on all matters whatsoever**." In other words, the British parliament insisted that it did have the right to govern the colonies (pass laws and levy taxes on them), even if the colonists didn't have a vote in their elections. Parliament declared this in 1766 with a new measure called the **Declaratory Act**.

The colonists, of course, did not believe that Parliament had such power over them. Parliament was elected by the people of Great Britain, not the colonists. This meant that Parliament represented the people of Great Britain, not the colonies. As a result, most colonists believed that Parliament did not have the right to rule (or tax) the colonies, except on the issue of trade, which Parliament had long had authority to manage (hence the Navigation Acts).

Parliament tried to enforce its power to rule over the colonies with a new set of taxes called the **Townshend Duties**. These were **tariffs** on goods the colonists bought from Britain, like paper, paint, glass, and tea. Parliament argued that since these items were imported to the colonies from Britain, they were trade goods and thus subject to Parliament's control. The Navigation Acts, they claimed, thus gave them the right to tax goods sent to the colonies.

The colonists acknowledged that the Navigation Acts did give Parliament the power to regulate (manage) trade within the British empire and that Parliament had long used tariffs or **duties** on imports to do so. However, past tariffs and duties were never meant to **raise revenue** (money). They were meant to persuade people to buy British made goods instead of foreign made goods. The tariffs and duties were only applied to foreign made goods, making them more expensive than English made goods. The Townshend Duties, however, were placed on British made goods.

The colonists argued that the only reason Parliament passed the new duties was to raise revenue (money) from them. In other words, it was a sneaky way for Parliament to tax the colonists, violating their slogan of No Taxation Without Representation".

As a result, calls for a **non-importation association** (boycott of the taxed goods) spread throughout the colonies.

Parliament was determined to enforce these new duties and sent two British regiments of troops to Boston to prevent disorder and protests. The colonists were angered by this, and on March 5, 1770, blood was shed when a large crowd in Boston, (some called it a mob), threatened a British sentry standing at his post. More British soldiers arrived to support the sentry. Some in the crowd threw snowballs and ice at the soldiers, prompting several to fire into the crowd. The incident, which killed and wounded several people in the crowd, became known as the **Boston Massacre**.

The British soldiers and their officer were charged with murder, but only two were convicted of manslaughter (unintentional killing) and given light punishments. Ironically, across the Atlantic Ocean, Parliament had given up on most of the Townshend Duties. The colonial boycott on the taxed goods and the expense of the two regiments of troops in Boston cost a lot more than the new duties ever collected. So, Parliament repealed all of the Townshend Duties except the tax on tea. It kept that tax as a symbol of its authority to tax (and rule) the colonists.

A tense calm settled over the British colonies in North America after the repeal of the Townshend Duties as most colonists hoped that Parliament had finally given up on their effort to govern and control them.

Unfortunately, Parliament had not.

Historical Timeline of the American Revolution

1754

July Battle of Fort Necessity – French and Indian War Begins

1762

Dec. *James Southall is Born*

1763

Feb. Treaty of Paris – French and Indian War Ends

Oct. Proclamation of 1763

Dec. *John Southall is Born*

1764

April Parliament Passes Sugar Act to Deter Colonial Smuggling

May *Rebecca Anderson is Born*

1765

Mar. Parliament Passes Stamp Act to Raise Revenue (Money)

May Patrick Henry's Stamp Act Resolves at Passed

1766

Mar. Parliament Repeals Stamp Act

Mar. Parliament Passes Declaratory Act

1767

July Parliament Passes Townshend Duties

1768

Oct. Parliament Sends British Troops to Boston

1769

May Virginians Adopt Non-Importation Association (Boycott)

1770

Mar.	Boston Massacre

1771

Mar.	*The Southall Family Buys the Raleigh Tavern*
Mar.	*The Anderson Family Leases Weatherburn's Tavern*
Sept.	John Murray, Earl of Dunmore (Lord Dunmore) Arrives in Williamsburg as Royal Governor

1772

June	British Ship *Gaspee* is destroyed by a Rhode Island Mob.

1773

Spring	Committees of Correspondence Form in the Colonies
May	Parliament Passes Tea Act
Dec.	Boston Tea Party

1774

Spring	Parliament Passes Intolerable Act
May	House of Burgesses Passes a Resolution of Prayer for Boston
May	Lord Dunmore Suspends the House of Burgesses
May	Ex-Burgesses Meet at the Raleigh Tavern; Call for a Boycott and Continental Congress
Aug.	First Virginia Convention Meets in Williamsburg
Sept.	First Continental Congress Meets in Philadelphia
Dec.	Lord Dunmore Returns from his Expedition Against the Shawnee

1775

Mar.	2nd Virginia Convention Meets – Patrick Henry Delivers his "Liberty or Death" Speech
April	Battle of Lexington and Concord
April	Williamsburg Gunpowder Incident
May	Patrick Henry Marches on Williamsburg
June	Lord Dunmore Flees Williamsburg
June	The Continental Congress Appoints George Washington as Commander-in-Chief of the Continental Army
Aug.	3rd Virginia Convention – Virginia Prepares for War
Oct.	Battle of Hampton
Nov.	Battle of Kemps Landing
Nov.	Lord Dunmore's Proclamation
Dec.	Battle of Great Bridge

1776

Jan.	Norfolk is Burned
May	5th Virginia Convention Votes for Independence
June	5th Virginia Convention Adopts New Constitution and Bill of Rights
July	Declaration of Independence
Aug.	Battle of Brooklyn
Sept.	British Capture New York
Dec.	Battle of Trenton

1777

Jan.	Battle of Princeton
Sept.	Battle of Brandywine
Sept.	British Capture Philadelphia
Sept./Oct.	Battle of Saratoga
Dec.	Valley Forge Encampment Begins

1778

June	Valley Forge Encampment Ends
June	Battle of Monmouth
Dec.	British Capture Savannah

1779

May	British Raid Virginia

1780

May	British Capture Charleston, South Carolina
May	Battle of the Waxhaws
Aug.	Battle of Camden
Sept.	Benedict Arnold Betrays America
Oct.	Battle of Kings Mountain
Oct./Nov.	British Raid Virginia
Dec.	Gen. Nathanael Greene Takes Command of American Southern Army
Dec.	Benedict Arnold Invades Virginia

1781

Jan.	Benedict Arnold Attacks Richmond
Jan.	Battle of Cowpens
Feb.	Race to the Dan
Mar.	Battle of Guilford Courthouse
April	Battle of Hobkirk Hill
April	Battle of Petersburg
April	General LaFayette Arrives in Virginia
May	General Cornwallis Arrives in Virginia
May/June	Siege of Ninety-Six
June/July	British Occupy Williamsburg
July	Battle of Green Spring
Sept./Oct.	Siege of Yorktown

Name ____________________ Date ____________

The 13 British Colonies

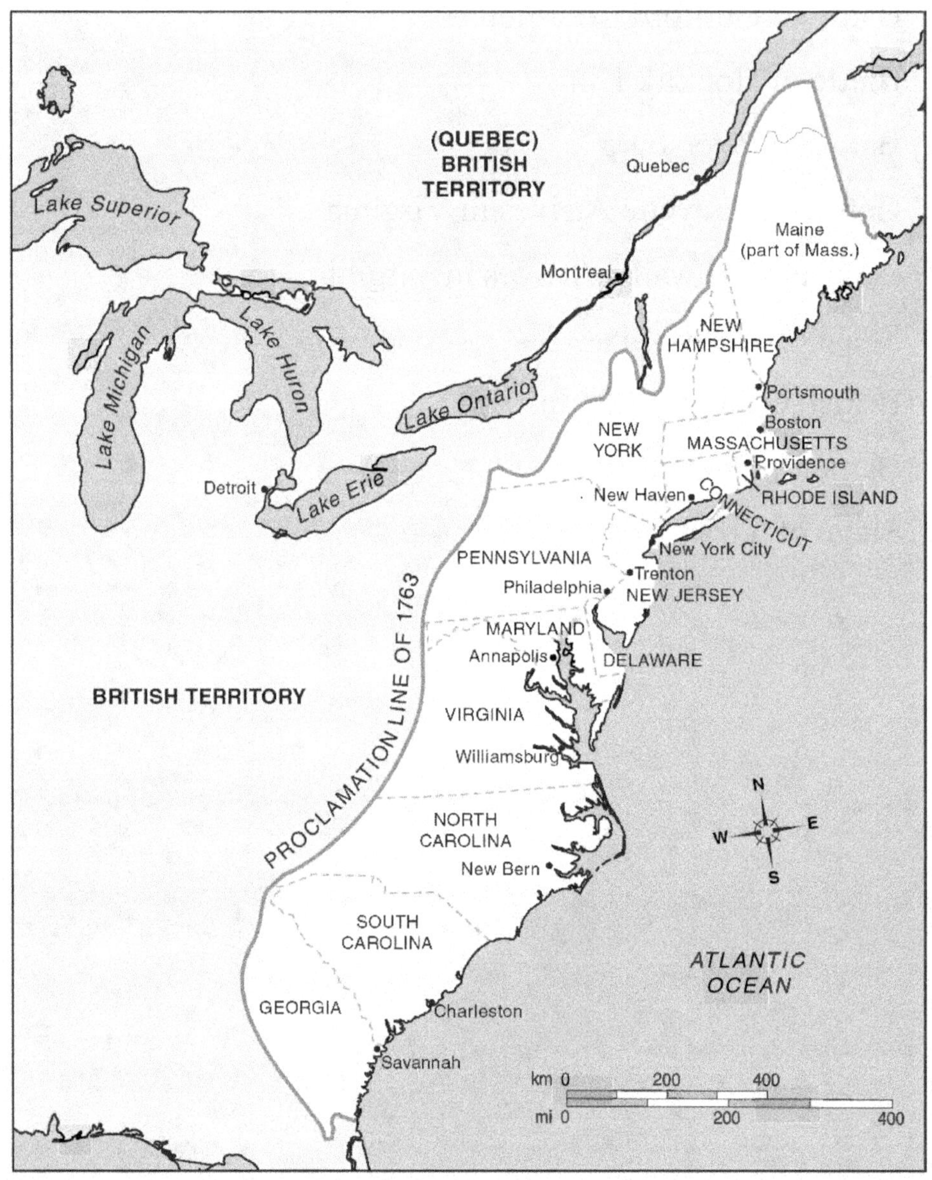

Useful Primary Source Accounts

Reactions to the Stamp Act

Richard Henry Lee to ------ , May 31, 1764

"***The right to be governed by laws made by our representatives***, *and* ***the illegality of taxation without consent*** *are such essential principles of the British constitution, that it is a...wonder how men, who have almost imbibed* [these principles since childhood] *should be of opinion that the people of America were to be taxed without consulting their representatives*."

Note: Lee wrote this letter in response to reports that the British parliament was considering the Stamp Act.

Source: James C. Ballagh, ed., "Richard Henry Lee to --- May 31, 1764," *The Letters of Richard Henry Lee*, Vol. 1, 5-6.

Petition of the Virginia General Assembly to King George III and Parliament December 18, 1764

It [is] *the fundamental Principle of the British Constitution without which Freedom can no Where exist, that* ***the People are not subject to any Taxes but such as are laid on them by their own Consent, or by those legally appointed to represent them***....

Note: The Virginia General Assembly was responding to the proposed Stamp Act.

Source: William J. Van Schreeven and Robert L. Scribner, eds., "Address, Memorial, and Remonstrance of the General Assembly to King, Lords and Commons Respectively in Opposition to a Proposed Stamp Tax, December 18, 1764," *Revolutionary Virginia: The Road to Independence*, Vol. 1, 11.

Patrick Henry's Stamp Act Resolve, May 30, 1765

"***The General Assembly of this Colony have the only and exclusive Right and Power to lay Taxes****...upon the inhabitants of this Colony and that every Attempt to vest such Power in any person or persons other than the General Assembly has a...Tendency to destroy British as well as American Freedom.*"

Source: William J. Van Schreeven and Robert L. Scribner, eds., "Resolutions Offered by Patrick Henry in Condemnation of the Stamp Act, May 29-30, 1765," *Revolutionary Virginia: The Road to Independence*, Vol. 1, 18.

Resolves Adopted by the Inhabitants of Norfolk, March 21, 1766

"***If we quietly submit to the execution of the Stamp Act, all our claims to civil liberties*** **[freedom]** ***will be lost, and we, and our posterity*** **[will]** ***become absolute slaves.***"

Source: Purdie and Dixon, *Virginia Gazette*, March 21 and April 4, 1766, 3.

George Washington to Francis Dandridge, Sept. 20, 1765

"[Virginians] *Look upon* ***this unconstitutional method of Taxation as a direful attack upon their Liberties****, and loudly exclaim against the Violations.*"

Source: W.W. Abbot and Dorothy Twohig, eds., "George Washington to Francis Dandridge, September 20, 1765," *The Papers of George Washington: Colonial Series*, Vol. 7, 395-396.

John Adams Diary, December 18, 1765

The Year 1765 has been the most remarkable Year of my Life. ***That enormous Engine, fabricated by the british Parliament, for battering down all the Rights and Liberties of America, I mean the Stamp Act,*** *has raised and spread, thro the whole Continent, a Spirit that will be recorded to our Honour, with all future Generations. In every Colony, from Georgia to New Hampshire inclusively, the Stamp*

Distributors and Inspectors have been compelled, by the unconquerable Rage of the People, to renounce their offices.

Such and ***so universal has been the Resentment of the People****, that every Man who has dared to speak in favour of the Stamps…has been seen to sink in universal Contempt and Ignominy. The People, even to the lowest Ranks, have become more attentive to their Liberties, more inquisitive about them, and more determined to defend them, than there were ever before known or had occasion to be….Our Presses have groaned, our Pulpits have thundered, our Legislatures have resolved, our Towns have voted, the Crown Officers have every where trembled, and all their little Tools and Creatures, been afraid to Speak and ashamed to be seen.*

Source: John Adams, Diary 11, Entry for Dec. 18, 1765, *Adams Family Papers*, Massachusetts Historical Society.

George Mason to the Committee of Merchants in London, June 6, 1766

"*Let our fellow-subjects in Great Britain reflect that* **we are descended from the same stock with themselves, nurtured in the same principles of freedom***…that in crossing the Atlantic Ocean, we have only changed our climate, not our minds, our natures and dispositions remain unaltered; that we are still the same people with them in every respect….* ***We claim nothing but the liberty and privileges of Englishmen, in the same degree, as if we still*** **[lived]** ***among our brethren in Great Britain;*** *these rights have not been forfeited by any act of ours; we cannot be deprived of them, without our consent, but by violence and injustice; we have received them from our ancestors, and, with God's leave, we will transmit them, unimpaired, to our posterity.*"

Source: Robert Rutland, ed., "To the Committee of Merchants in London, June 6, 1766," *The Papers of George Mason*, Vol. 1, 68

The Declaratory Act, March 18, 1766

"***The said colonies***...*in America have been,* ***are, and of right ought to be, subordinate unto, and dependent upon the imperial crown and Parliament*** *of Great Britain; and that* ***the king...with the advice and consent of...Parliament...hath...full power and authority to make laws...to bind the colonies and people of America,*** *subjects of the crown of Great Britain*, ***in all cases whatsoever***."

Source: Henry Steele Commager, ed., "The Declaratory Act, March 18, 1766," *Documents of American History*, 60-61.

Reaction to the Townshend Duties, 1768

Petition to the British Parliament from the Virginia House of Burgesses, April 16, 1768

"***To say that the Parliament of Great Britain has the constitutional Authority and Right to impose internal Taxes on the Inhabitants of this Continent, who are not and...cannot be Represented in the house of Commons, is...to command them to bid Adieu to their natural and civil Liberties and prepare for a state of Slavery***."

Source: William J. Van Schreeven and Robert L. Scribner, eds., "To the Right Honorable, The Spiritual and Temporal In Parliament Assembled, April 16, 1768," *Revolutionary Virginia: The Road to Independence*, Vol. 1, 58.

Reactions to the Intolerable Acts 1774

An Association Signed by 89 Members of the late House of Burgesses, May 27, 1774

"*We are further clearly of opinion,* ***that an attack made on one of our sister colonies, to compel submission to arbitrary taxes, is an attack made on all British America****, and* ***threatens ruin to the rights of all****, unless the united wisdom of the* *whole be applied. And for this purpose it is recommended…*[that] *deputies from the several colonies of British America meet in general congress.*"

Source: William J. Van Schreeven and Robert L. Scribner, eds., "An Association Signed by 89 Members of the late House of Burgesses, May 27, 1774," *Revolutionary Virginia: The Road to Independence*, Vol. 1, 97-98.

Edmund Pendleton to Joseph Chew, June 20, 1774

"*Tho' it should be granted that* ***the Bostonians did wrong in destroying the tea****, yet* ***the Parliament giving Judgement and sending ships and troops to*** [punish the entire city] *in a case of Private property* ***is [an] Attack upon constitutional Rights****, of which we could not remain Idle Spectators….*"

Source: David John Mays, ed., "Edmund Pendleton to Joseph Chew, June 20, 1774," *The Letters and Papers of Edmund Pendleton*, Vol. 1, 93.

Col. George Washington to Bryan Fairfax, July 3, 1774

"*As to your political* [loyalist] *sentiments, I would heartily join you in them…provided there was the most distant hope of success. But have we not tried this already? Have we not addressed* [Parliament]? *And to what end? Did* [Parliament] *deign to look at our petitions?* ***Does it not appear, as clear as*** **[the sun]*…that there is a regular, systematic plan formed to fix the right and practice of taxation upon us?*** *Does not the uniform conduct of Parliament for some years confirm this… Is there anything to be expected from petitioning after this?…* ***Is not the attack upon the liberty and property of the people of Boston…plain and self-evident proof of what they are aiming at***?"

Source: Beverly H. Runge, ed., "George Washington to Bryan Fairfax, July 4, 1774," *The Papers of George Washington: Colonial Series*, Vol. 10, 109-110.

Col. George Washington to Bryan Fairfax, July 20, 1774

"*For Sir, what is it we are contending against? Is it against paying the duty of three pence per pound on tea because* [it is] *burthensome? No, it is the right only, we have all along disputed* ***.... I think the Parliament of Great Britain hath no more right to put their hands into my pockets, without my consent, than I have to put my hands into yours for money****; and this being already urged to them in a firm, but decent manner, by all the colonies, what reason is there to expect anything from their justice*?"

Source: Beverly H. Runge, ed., "George Washington to Bryan Fairfax, July 20, 1774," *The Papers of George Washington: Colonial Series*, Vol. 10, 129.

Patrick Henry's Liberty or Death Speech (excerpted) March 23, 1775

"***Are fleets and armies necessary...*****[for]** ***reconciliation****? Have we shown ourselves so unwilling to be reconciled, that force must be called in to win back our love? Let us not deceive ourselves, sir.* ***These are the implements of war and subjugation*** *– the last arguments to which kings resort.... I ask gentlemen, sir, what means this martial array, if its purpose be not to force us to submission... Has Great Britain any enemy in this quarter of the world, to call for all this accumulation of navies and armies? No, sir, she had none. They are meant for us, they can be meant for no other.* ***They are sent over to bind and rivet upon us those chains which the British ministry have be so long forging****...In vain, after these* [appeals and petitions] *may we indulge the fond hope of peace and reconciliation. There is no longer any room for hope****. If we wish to be free...we must fight!*** *I repeat it, sir, we must fight!...* ***There is no retreat, but into submission and slavery! Our chains are forged. Their***

clanking may be heard on the plains of Boston! The war is inevitable *– and let it come! I repeat it sir, let it come! It is in vain, sir, to extenuate the matter. Gentlemen may cry, peace, peace – but there is no peace. The war is actually begun! The next gale that sweeps from the north will bring to our ears the clash of resounding arms! Our brethren are already in the field! Why stand we here idle? What is it that gentlemen wish? What would they have****? Is life so dear, or peace so sweet as to be purchased at the price of chains and slavery? Forbid it, Almighty God! I know not what course others may take; but as for me, give me liberty, or give me death***!"

Source: William Wirt, *Sketches in the Life and Character of Patrick Henry*, 136-141.

George Washington Reacts to his Appointment as Commander of the Continental Army

Gen. George Washington to Burwell Bassett, June 19, 1775

"***I am now Imbarked on a tempestuous Ocean*** *from whence, perhaps, no friendly harbor is to be found. I have been called by the unanimous Voice of the Colonies to the Command of the Continental Army – It is an honour I by no means aspired to –* ***It is an honour I wished to avoid, as well from an unwillingness to quit the peaceful enjoyment of my Family as from a thorough conviction of my own Incapacity & want of experience in the conduct of so momentous a concern****."*

Source: Philander D. Chase, ed., "George Washington to Burwell Bassett, June 19, 1775," *The Papers of George Washington: Revolutionary War Series*, Vol. 1, 12-13.

1776: Facing Defeat Along the Delaware River

General Washington to Samuel Washington, Dec. 18, 1776

"I have no doubt that General Howe will still make an attempt upon Philadelphia this Winter. I see nothing to oppose him in a fortnight from this time, as the term of all the Troops except those of Virginia…[and] Maryland…will expire in that time. **In a word my dear Sir, if every nerve is not strain'd to recruit the New Army with all possible expedition, I think the game is pretty near up**."

Source: Philander D. Chase, ed., "George Washington to Samuel Washington, December 18, 1776," *The Papers of George Washington: Revolutionary War Series*, Vol. 7, 370.

Impact of the Battle of Trenton: 1776

Nicholas Cresswell Journal Entry, January 1777

"News that Washington had taken 760 Hessian prisoners at Trenton…is confirmed… **The minds of the people are much altered. A few days ago they had given up the cause for lost. Their late success have turned the scale and now they are all liberty mad again**. Their Recruiting parties could not get a man…and now the men are coming in by companies. Confound the [Hessians]… This has given them new spirits, got them fresh succours [support], and will prolong the war, perhaps for two years."

Source: *The Diary of Nicholas Cresswell*, 179-180.

Witness to Revolution (1771-1777)

Notable People

George Washington
George Wythe
Lord Dunmore
Lord Botetourt
Robert Carter Nicholas
Lord Fincastle
Charles Scott
Gen. Thomas Gage
John Locke
Patrick Henry
Peyton Randolph
John Southall
George Mason
John Randolph
Betsy Farrow
Col. William Woodford
Gen. William Howe
Thomas Paine
Thomas Jefferson
King George III
Robert Anderson
Richard Henry Lee
Edmund Pendleton
Benjamin Harrison
Gen. Charles Lee
Gen. John Burgoyne

Important Terms, Places, and Events

French & Indian War
Stamp Act (Tax)
"No Taxation Without Representation
Non-Importation Association 1769 (boycott)
Boston Massacre
Boston Tea Party
Non-Importation Association 1774 (boycott)
First Continental Congress
Lexington & Concord
Williamsburg Gunpowder Incident
War Debt
Declaratory Act
Tar & Feather
Townshend Duties
Tea Act
Coercive/Intolerable Acts
"Liberty or Death
Militia
British Regulars
Continental Regulars

Congress Appoints George Washington Commanding General

Patrick Henry's March on Williamsburg

Lord Dunmore Flees Williamsburg

Battle of Kemps Landing

Lord Dunmore's Proclamation

Virginia Vote for Independence

Battle of Gwynn's Island

Battles of Trenton & Princeton

British Capture Philadelphia

Smallpox Inoculation

Battle of Bunker Hill

Battle of Hampton

Battle of Great Bridge

Burning of Norfolk

Declaration of Independence

British Capture New York City

Battle of Saratoga

Cherokee Peace Delegation

Guided Reading Questions for *Witness to Revolution*

Directions: Based on your reading, answer the questions below on a separate sheet of paper with as much detail as possible.

Chapter One

1. What are your first impressions of James, John, and Rebecca.
   Describe their personalities. Identify the traits that you share with each of them.

Chapter Two

1. What were taverns in colonial days?
   What businesses are similar to colonial taverns today?

2. Why did women rarely stay overnight in a tavern?

3. What was so special about the Raleigh Tavern?

4. What important event happened in the Apollo Room of the Raleigh in 1769?

5. Why was it so important to know how to dance well in Virginia?

Chapter Three

1. What types of events or activities attracted the most visitors to Williamsburg each year?
   How did the taverns benefit from this?

2. What activity occurred regularly in front of the Raleigh Tavern that so upset Rebecca?
   Why did this activity not bother James or John the first time Rebecca saw it?

3. What was Christmastime like in Williamsburg / Virginia?
   Describe the activities and atmosphere of the time.
   How was it different from today?

Chapter Four

1. What did James and many older, more conservative burgesses think about Patrick Henry?

2. What did John think about Patrick Henry?

3. Explain what Patrick Henry and others meant by the slogan, “No Taxation Without Representation?
   Based on the slogan, who could not tax us and why?

4. According to Mr. Henry and his supporters, what did the colonists risk becoming if we let Parliament get away with taxing us?
   Explain why we would be reduced to such a state?

5. How did Colonel George Washington feel about the issue?

6. What role did enslaved people have in the operation of the Raleigh and Anderson taverns?

Chapter Five

1. What was the purpose of creating a committee of correspondence in 1773 and why was it so important?

2. Describe James’s experience at William and Mary?
   Why was he treated the way he was?

3. Describe how Virginians reacted to the news of the Boston Tea Party?
   Use at least one specific quote to support your description.

4. Why were many Virginians concerned about the Tea Party incident?

5. What did John think about the Boston Tea Party?

Chapter Six

1. How did the arrival of Lord Dunmore's children impact James at school?
   Why do you think little Lord Fincastle acted the way he did?

2. How did Mr. George Wythe help James?
   Why did Mr. Wythe's actions help?

3. When James asked whether the colonists were obliged to help pay for part of Britain's huge debt, what did Mr. Wythe and Mr. Jefferson say? What was the key point to them?

4. What was the Declaratory Act?
   What did Parliament claim the act allowed them to do?

5. Why did Mr. Wythe and Mr. Jefferson think the Declaratory Act was so dangerous?

6. Summarize Mr. Wythe's view about who had the right to tax the colonist and why.

Chapter Seven

1. Why was Patrick Henry glad that Bostonians dumped tea into their harbor?

2. How did the British Parliament react to the news of the Boston Tea Party?
   What did they do to Boston / Massachusetts?

3. How did most Virginians react to Parliament's response to the Tea Party?
   What did they say about it? What did they do about it?

4. How did Lord Dunmore react to the Day of Prayer resolution passed by the House of Burgesses in May 1774 to support the suffering people of Boston.
   Use his actual words in your answer.

5. Where did the dismissed burgesses meet after Lord Dunmore dissolved the House of Burgesses?

6. What important decision was made by these men at their meeting?

Chapter Eight

1. What did the Virginia Convention do in August 1774 and why was this so important?

2. What did the Continental Congress agree to do to help / support Massachusetts in 1774?
   How was this policy actually supposed to help the people of Massachusetts?

3. How was this new policy **enforced** in the colonies. Be specific.
   What kind of consequences might someone who violated the new policy expect?

4. Who did Lord Dunmore defeat in 1774 and how did the residents of Williamsburg react when he returned?

5. Why was Lord Dunmore so displeased by the discovery of an independent militia company in Williamsburg?

Chapter Nine

1. What was so unique about the William Pitman murder case?

2. Why was John so conflicted about this case?

3. What happened at the Gunpowder Magazine in Williamsburg on April 21, 1775?

4. How did the residents of Williamsburg react to this incident?

5. Why were they so concerned about it?

6. Who did most residents of Williamsburg blame for the incident and who helped peacefully settle the crisis, at least temporarily?

7. What shocking news reached Williamsburg in late April about Massachusetts?
   What was the British army trying to seize in Concord?

8. Who almost caused fighting and bloodshed in Williamsburg in early May 1775 and what did he do to almost cause it?

9. What did Governor Dunmore and his family do in early June 1775? Why?

10. Who was placed in command of the American army in Massachusetts in the summer of 1775?
    Why did Congress pick him?

11. What did James and his friend William Worley disagree about?
    What did they agree on?

12. How did the militia volunteers who camped in Williamsburg in the summer of 1775 cause a problem?

13. What is the difference between militia and regular soldiers?
    How many regulars did Virginia recruit in the fall of 1775?

14. What does the fact that Virginia recruited so many regular soldiers imply about their expectations with the dispute with Britain?

Chapter Ten

1. If you were a visitor to Williamsburg in the fall of 1775, what would you have seen?
    What was happening in the town that was both exciting and worrisome?

2. Who commanded the 1st Virginia Regiment of regulars and why was his selection so controversial to some?

3. What did James, John, and Rebecca see when they visited the army camp behind the college?

4. Identify the main weapon of 18th century warfare and why training and discipline were so important for using it.

5. What were some of the problems and challenges a Virginia soldier faced in 1775?

6. Where did the first battle in Virginia with the British happen?
   What was the British navy trying to do? Did they succeed?

7. What did Lord Dunmore order his small force of 120 British redcoats to take every chance they got?

8. What shocking news from Philadelphia reached Williamsburg in early November?

9. After his victory at Kemp's Landing, Governor Dunmore issued a very important proclamation. What did the proclamation say and how did people react to it?
   Who liked the proclamation and who didn't like it?

10, In late November, Rebecca faced a very difficult choice. Describe the situation and the choice she made.
   Why was it such a hard choice for her?

11. What happened at the Battle of Great Bridge in early December?
   Who won? How did the result of the battle impact support for Dunmore and his plan to use Norfolk as a base of operation?

Chapter Eleven

1. What happened to Norfolk at the beginning of 1776?
   Who was blamed for it?

2. What did the English philosopher John Locke say was the purpose of government?

3. What subject was discussed more and more in 1776 because of all the bloodshed and destruction of 1775?

4. Why do you think John found the writings of Thomas Paine exciting while James thought Mr. Paine was too extreme in his views?

5. How did Rebecca feel about independence from Britain in 1776?
Did this surprise you? Why or why not?

6. Summarize why James and John believed that the British Parliament was to blame for all the talk about independence.

7. Why was James more cautious and careful about calling for independence?

8. Why was John so confident that the colonies could win their independence from Britain?

9. Why did Patrick Henry resign from the army in 1776?

10. What did Patrick Henry do to help de-fuse a crisis that arose when he resigned from the army?

11. Why did James compliment Mr. Henry about his actions?

12. What important event happened in Williamsburg on May 15, 1776 and what did Rebecca think about it?

Chapter Twelve

1. After May 15th, the 5th Virginia Convention turned its attention to writing a new constitution (plan for government). What did George Mason insist be added to this new constitution?

2. How do you think a Declaration of Rights would actually protect the people?

3. According to Mr. Mason, (who borrowed his ideas from John Locke) government power came from where? What did Mr. Mason think should be done with the power government was given to prevent the government from abusing it?

4. Why was John thrilled by the election of Virginia's new governor?

5. What happened on Gwynn's Island in July that was so important?

6. What did the departure of Lord Dunmore from Virginia after Gwynn's Island allow Virginia to do with many of its soldiers?

7. What happened to James's friend, William Wormley?
   Why did this happen?

8. What happened in the fall of 1776 in New York that concerned James, John, and Rebecca?

9. What happened to General Washington's army during this time period? (Fall 1776)

10. Describe the condition of General Washington's army in December 1776 along the Delaware River.

11. How did General Washington drastically turn the situation around against the British on Christmas night and the next day?
    What challenges did they overcome?

12. What was the impact of General Washington's victories at Trenton and Princeton?

Chapter Thirteen

1. What disease spread among both armies in 1776-77?
   Why did such a disease spread so fast in armies?

2. What did General Washington do to try to stop it from spreading?

3. What was it like to have smallpox?

4. What was a benefit of being inoculated for smallpox?

5. Who came to Williamsburg in the summer of 1777 to finalize a peace treaty with Virginia?
   Why do you think they fought the Virginians in 1776?

6. What defeats and setbacks did the Americans suffer in 1777?

7. What happened at the Battle of Saratoga in 1777 and why was it so important?

8. How did the residents of Williamsburg react to the news of Saratoga?

9. Why did John get so mad at the things he overheard some gentlemen say in the Raliegh Tavern about General Washington?

10. Who surprised everyone at the Capitol Ball in honor of Saratoga?

11. John and James's view of Rebecca changed because of the Capitol Ball. Why do you think this happened?

12. What was Rebecca's biggest concern as 1777 came to an end?

Big Idea Questions

Explain why leaders like Patrick Henry, Thomas Jefferson, George Wythe, and believed it was wrong for the British Parliament to tax (or try to rule) the colonists?

What did the colonists risk becoming if Parliament succeeded in ruling over the colonists with new taxes and policies? Why would this be accurate?

If you had to explain to someone who had no knowledge about the American Revolution, what would you say was the main reason or reasons the colonists rebelled against Great Britain?

Map of Revolutionary War Battles in the South

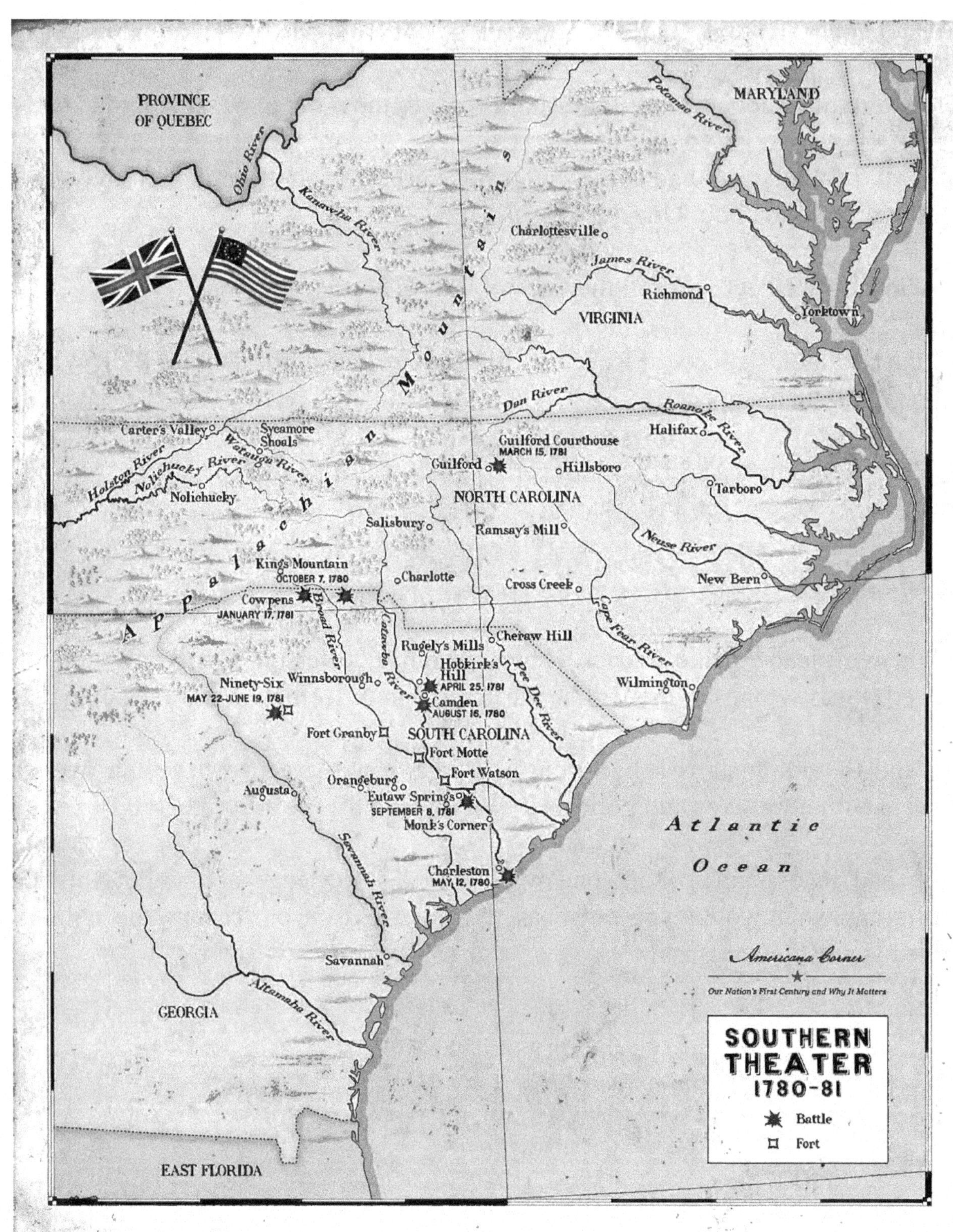

Witness to War (1778-1780)

Important People

George Washington
Patrick Henry
Thomas Jefferson
Col. John Dixon
Capt. James Southall
Capt. Robert Anderson
Gen. Thomas Nelson
Gen. Henry Clinton
Henry Hamilton
Col. Abraham Buford
Gen. William Woodford
Col. Banastre Tarleton
Gen. Benjamin Lincoln
Capt. Adam Wallace
Col. Charles Porterfield
Gen. Baron de Kalb
Gen. Horatio Gates
Gen. Nathanael Greene
Gen. Danial Morgan
Capt. Andrew Wallace
Gen. Peter Muhlenberg
Col. Patrick Ferguson
Gen. Alexander Leslie
Gen. Charles Cornwallis
Gen. Benedict Arnold

Important Terms, Places, and Events

Battle of Saratoga
Occupation of Philadelphia
Valley Forge
Virginia General Assembly
Militia Troops
Continental Army
College Company
Battle of Monmouth
Recruitment Bounties
French Alliance
British Capture Savannah
Siege of Savannah
Capital Moves to Richmond
British Legion
Siege of Charleston
Battle of the Waxhaws
Hillsborough, NC
Battle of Camden
Battle of Kings Mountain
Gen. Leslie's Raid on Virginia
Camp Followers

Guided Reading Questions for *Witness to War*

Directions: Based on your reading, answer the questions below on a separate sheet of paper with as much detail as possible.

Note: At the end of the first book, Witness to Revolution, James, John, and Rebecca attended their first ball in Williamsburg. It was a grand affair, especially for Rebecca.

Chapter One

According to the second book, *Witness to War*...

1. What was the reason Williamsburg's leaders held a ball in November 1777?

2. How was the good news about Saratoga offset by news from Pennsylvania?

3. Why do you think Rebecca received so much new attention on her way to church a few days after the ball?

4. What did Rebecca do after church that surprised both James and John?

5. What did John do at the brook, their favorite gathering spot, that annoyed Rebecca?

    - For those who read the first book, what do you think the title of chapter one in the second book refers to?

Chapter Two

1. Explain what the title of chapter two refers to.

2. Why were Continental officers in Williamsburg in the winter of 1778?

3. Where was General Washington's army encamped in the winter of 1778 and what was life like for the soldiers there?

4. Why were the Continental officers in Williamsburg so discouraged?

5. What exciting news arrived from across the Atlantic in May and why was John so encouraged by it?

6. What other good news lifted American morale in the summer of 1778?

Chapter Three

1. According to James and John, name several ways Virginia's government was the same and several ways it was different since the Declaration of Independence in July 1776.

2. What challenges did James and his college company of student militia face in 1778?

3. What challenges did the city militia of Williamsburg under Colonel Dixon and Captain Southall face in 1778?

Chapter Four

1. What good news from Europe reached Virginia in early 1779?

2. How did the arrival of British troops in Virginia in May 1779 impact James and the College Company?
   What did they do?

3. Describe the experience that James and his fellow soldiers in the College Company had in 1779 when they took the field and marched to Smithfield.
   What problems, challenges, shortages, did they face?

4. What role did James play with the College Company during their march to Smithfield and back?

5. What did James learn about being a soldier during his time in the field with the militia in May 1779?

Chapter Five

1. What shocking decision did Governor Jefferson and the state legislature make concerning the capital after the British raid on Virginia in May 1779?

2. Why did Rebecca's father and many others in Williamsburg dismiss the likelihood of the government actually leaving Williamsburg?

3. Why was Henry Hamilton called the "Hair Buyer" and what was his time in Williamsburg like for him?

4. What opportunity presented itself to James after his graduation from William and Mary and why was his father so pleased about it?

5. What happens to the price of goods when there is high inflation and what caused such high inflation in Virginia by 1779?

Chapter Six

1. Describe James's situation with the Nelson family after his graduation from college. Be sure to include:

   What his new title was (his job).
   How he was treated.
   Why he was well suited (a good choice) for the job.

Chapter Seven

1. Why was John so discouraged about the war near the end of 1779?

2. What was Rebecca's main concern regarding John's 16th birthday?

3. What stunning news did James receive from Rebecca a few weeks after Christmas?

   Why were both James and Rebecca so upset about it?

Chapter Eight

1. What decision did John make in early 1780 and why did Rebecca disagree with it?

2. How did John compare with the other Continental soldiers?

3. What did John's fellow Continentals think about his decision to enlist in the Continental army instead of staying with the militia?

4. Why do you think John chose the Continentals over the militia?

5. What problems did the Continentals face in Petersburg?

Chapter Nine

1. How long of a journey was it to travel from Williamsburg to Richmond in the 18th century?

2. Why was John's detachment of Continentals delayed in marching south to join the rest of the American southern army in Charleston, South Carolina?

Chapter Ten

1. Who commanded John's detachment of Continentals and who commanded his particular company?

2. Identify some of the new lessons, or shortcuts, John learned about army life as time went by.

3. Describe the size and look (clothing) of Colonel Abraham Buford's detachment of Continentals that marched south from Petersburg in late March, 1780.

4. Describe their sleeping situation on the march.

5. Explain who camp followers were and how did John feel about them.

6. Why did Colonel Buford reverse direction and head back to Virginia in late May?

7. Describe in detail what happened to John and his fellow Continentals on May 29, 1780 at the Waxhaws.

    Be sure to include:

    Who attacked them.
    What mistakes Colonel Buford made.
    What happened to Burford's Continentals in the battle.
    What happened to John specifically.

Chapter Eleven

1. When John first approached a family for help after the battle, what was he afraid of?

2. Identify and describe John's wounds.

3. Explain how Mr. and Mrs. Cain helped John.

4. Describe John's journey to Salisbury.
    How far away was Salisbury?
    How did John get there and how long did it take?
    Who did he meet there and where did he go next?

5. What happened to John's commander, Captain Wallace, and the rest of his company?

6. What shocking sight did John encounter when he reported to a doctor in Salisbury?

7. How did John get to Hillsborough, North Carolina?

8. John arrived in Hillsborough very sick and was immediately placed in quarantine. What illness did John have and who helped him get to the house he was quarantined in?

Chapter Twelve

1. How did Rebecca and her family do in their new tavern in Richmond in 1780?

2. Who was Abigail Jenkins and how did she help John through his illness?

3. Who was Colonel Charles Porterfield and how did he help John once he had recovered from smallpox?

4. Summarize Colonel Porterfield's military experience prior to 1780.

5. With most of his original unit destroyed at the Waxhaws and the remnants back in Virginia, what did John decide to do in late June?

Chapter Thirteen

1. Describe the challenges the American southern army faced as it marched to South Carolina in the summer of 1780.

2. The battle of Camden actually began with a night engagement. Describe in detail what happened that night and particularly what happened to Colonel Porterfield and John.

3. What happened to the American army at Camden the next morning and who was largely to blame?

Chapter Fourteen

1. After John returned to Hillsborough with the remnants of the American southern army, what did he spend a lot of his time doing?

2. Who joined the army in Hillsborough in early October and took command of the light infantry troops, which included John and his new company under Captain Andrew Wallace?

3. What was the one drawback for John about being assigned to General Morgan's light corps?

Chapter Fifteen

1. How did General Nelson surprise James in October 1780 when the British returned to Virginia?

2. What responsibilities did James have as an aide to General Nelson?

3. Why did British plans in Virginia suddenly change? Explain what happened in South Carolina in early October that caused the change.

4. Who took charge of the American southern army in early December 1780.

5. Why did this new commander send General Morgan and his light corps into western South Carolina in late December.

6. Who was on his way to Virginia at the same time, sent by the British commander in New York, General Henry Clinton?

Big Idea Question

Describe what life as an American soldier (either as a continental or a militiaman) was really like as the war stretched on and on.

Witness to Victory (1781)

Important People

Gen. Benedict Arnold
Gen. Thomas Nelson
Gen. Daniel Morgan
Col. Banaster Tarleton
Gen. Nathanael Greene
Col. "Light Horse" Harry Lee
Gen. Marquis de LaFayette
Col. John Simcoe
Gen. Rochambeau
Gov. Thomas Jefferson
Benjamin Harrison
Capt. Andrew Wallace
Col. John Howard
Gen. Charles Cornwallis
Gen. William Phillips
Gen. Anthony Wayne
Col. James Innes

Important Terms, Places, and Events

Arnold Invades Virginia
German Jagers
Ninety-Six, SC
Battle of Cowpens
Battle of Guilford Courthouse
Battle of Petersburg
Point of Fork, VA
Battle of Green Spring
Westover, VA
Richmond, VA
Camden, SC
Race to the Dan
Portsmouth, VA
Petersburg, VA
Monticello, VA
Siege of Yorktown
Arnold Attacks Richmond
Simcoe's Queen's Rangers
Tarleton's Legion
Light Infantry Corps
Battle of Hobkirk Hill
Charlottesville, VA
Siege of Ninety-Six

Guided Reading Questions for *Witness to Victory*

Directions: Based on your reading, answer the questions below on a separate sheet of paper with as much detail as possible.

Chapter One

1. Who was Benedict Arnold and who did he bring with him to Virginia in December 1780?

2. How did news of Arnold's arrival disrupt the plans of James?

3. How did Virginia's leaders in the new capital of Richmond react to the news of the British arrival?

4. How did James help?

5. When James finally left Richmond to join General Nelson, he had to turn around and return to the capital. What caused him to do so?

Chapter Two

1. What dilemma did Rebecca and her family face with the British getting closer and closer to Richmond?

2. Why did they stay and what did they do to prepare for the British?

3. What mission did James and Major Anderson undertake in the evening?

4. What happened during this mission?

Chapter Three

1. Describe the battle that occurred in Richmond. Be sure to include:

   Who fought? Where was the militia posted at the beginning of the battle? Who won the battle? What did James do in the battle?

2. How would you describe Rebecca's conduct towards Benedict Arnold? Why do you think she acted this way?

3. What did Rebecca, with the help of Ben, try to do while General Arnold and his officers dined at the Anderson's tavern?

Chapter Four

1. What did General Arnold do with the public buildings in Richmond before he left? Explain why you think he did this.

2. How did Arnold's actions impact Rebecca and her family?

3. Who helped save some of the items inside the Anderson's tavern? What things were saved?

4. How did General Arnold respond to the fire that burned Rebecca's home?

5. Describe how the Andersons adjusted to the loss of their tavern.

6. If you were Rebecca's father or mother, what would you say to her about her conduct while Arnold was in Richmond?

Chapter Five

1. Describe the situation of the militia under General Nelson that James discovered when he finally joined General Nelson in January 1781.

2. What did Rebecca's parents decide to do about the loss of their tavern?

3. How had seventeen-year-old John Southall's attitude about war changed during his first year with the army? Why do you think it changed?

4. Describe the difference between most Continental and militia soldiers.

5. Why did 18th century armies usually go into winter quarters during the wintertime? In other words, why was it so hard for 18th century armies to remain in the field in the winter? Hint: It has something to do with their animals.

6. Why did General Greene split the American army in late December, 1780?

7. Explain why the American light infantry under General Daniel Morgan, with whom John Southall was attached, was in significant danger in January 1781.

8. What smart action did General Morgan repeatedly do with the militia the night before the Battle of Cowpens.
   What did he ask the militia to do in the upcoming fight?

Chapter Six

1. Why did General Morgan's plan suddenly change on the morning of January 17 at Cowpens?

2. What expectations did John have for the militia? Why did he have little confidence in them?

3. How did the American militia actually do in the battle? Did they meet General Morgan's expectations?

4. Describe the fighting John experienced in the third American line at Cowpens.

5. Why did John and his fellow Virginians suddenly withdraw towards the rear during the battle?

6. How did the Americans manage to win the Battle of Cowpens?

7. What happened to most of Colonel Tarleton's British troops at Cowpens?

8. How did John show mercy and compassion to the enemy?

Chapter Seven

1. How effective was Virginia's militia against Benedict Arnold's force in Virginia and where did Arnold post his army for a few months?

2. What problems confronted Virginia's militia during Arnold's stay.

3. Where did James and General Nelson stay in the winter of 1781 and who was James surprised to see there one day?

4. How did Rebecca help the American cause and why was this dangerous for her?

5. What did Rebecca say about Benedict Arnold to James?

Chapter Eight

1. Describe John's mixed feelings about the Battle of Cowpens.

2. Why did General Greene decide to retreat to Virginia?

3. What role did John and the American light corps play in the retreat? What was their mission?

4. Describe what the Race to the Dan was like for John and his fellow American soldiers.

Chapter Nine

1. Describe Rebecca's activities in Williamsburg while the militia was posted there.

2. Who was General Marquis de LaFayette and why did he arrive in Virginia?

3. Explain how General Greene borrowed the same tactic that General Morgan used at Cowpens for his battle at Guilford Courthouse.
   Where were John and his fellow Virginians posted?

4. Describe what happened in the Battle of Guilford Courthouse.
   Be sure to include:
      How the American army was deployed for battle?
      Where John was posted and what happened to him?
      How the battle ended and who won?

5. Who was John surprised to see in camp after the battle and why was she there?

6. What happened in Virginia in late March to ruin American hopes to capture Benedict Arnold?

Chapter Ten

1. How did the situation in Williamsburg change dramatically in the middle of April, 1781.

2. What did James and the militia do when the British landed near Williamsburg?

3. What did Rebecca do? Why?

4. Describe Rebecca's encounter with Benedict Arnold.

5. Describe what the British army did to the town during their brief stay in Williamsburg.

Chapter Eleven

1. Why was John so admired by many of the soldiers in his new company?

2. Why was John so upset about the Battle of Hobkirk Hill in Camden, South Carolina?

3. What duty was John happily assigned to after the battle? Why did this please him?

4. Who arrived in Virginia in late April with reinforcements from General Washington's main army? How many troops did he have with him?

5. Who assumed command of all the British troops in Virginia in mid-May?

Chapter Twelve

1. Describe what an 18th century siege involved and why General Greene decided to begin one upon the British outpost at Ninety-Six.

2. Explain why General Greene's siege began poorly. What mistake did he make?

3. What was the Siege of Ninety-Six like for John and his fellow soldiers?

Chapter Thirteen

1. How did General LaFayette foil General Cornwallis's main objective and where did Cornwallis turn his attention to attack instead?

2. What happened to General Nelson in mid-June and how did this impact James?

3. What unusual (unorthodox) tactics did General Greene try during his Siege of Ninety-Six?

4. Describe in detail, the final American attack on Ninety-Six. Why did General Greene launch it?

5. Describe what happened to John in this attack?

Chapter Fourteen

1. Describe what happened in Williamsburg when General Cornwallis and the British army arrived in the city in late June.

2. How did Rebecca and many of Williamsburg's residents react to the arrival of the British army in their city?

3. Describe what happened at the Battle of Green Spring and James's role in it. Why was the battle almost a disaster for the Americans?

Chapter Fifteen

1. Describe John's reaction to his realization of what happened to him in the attack on Ninety-Six.
   What was his concern?

2. Who saved John from the battle?

3. When did John finally begin to believe that he'd be alright despite his wound?

4. What surprising news did General LaFayette share with his officers about General Washington?

5. How did James inform John of the news about General Washington and what did John do in response?

Chapter Sixteen

1. What did General Washington's plan to trap General Cornwallis in Yorktown depend on?

2. Describe what Williamsburg was like in September 1781, just prior to the Siege of Yorktown.

3. Describe the reunion of James, John, and Rebecca.
   Where/how did it happen?

4. Whose command was James transferred to before the siege at Yorktown? Why do you think he was transferred?

5. Explain how John found hope in Abigail's past experience with her injury.

6. What did General Washington remember and ask James when James saw the General at headquarters at Mr. Wythe's house?

Chapter Seventeen

1. Describe the size of the British, French, and American armies at Yorktown.

2. What made General Cornwallis decide to abandon most of his isolated outer works (forts) that ringed Yorktown.

3. Describe the Siege of Yorktown in detail.
   What did the allies do?
   What was Cornwallis hoping for?

4. Identify key events that occurred during the siege.

5. Describe the British surrender at Yorktown.
   If you were watching it, what would you have seen?

Chapter Eighteen

1. How did the surrender of Cornwallis and his British army at Yorktown impact the American states and Great Britain?

2. What document officially ended the war and when was it signed?

3. How long did the Revolutionary War last?

4. Describe how James, John, Rebecca, and Abigail felt about the future in the weeks after Yorktown.

Big Idea Questions

If you had to describe what the Revolutionary War was like in 1781, what would you say?

Be sure to include:

What were the most important battles?

What was it like to serve in the American Southern army in 1781 under General Morgan and General Greene?

What was it like to be in Richmond and Williamsburg when the British arrived?

What was it like to be at Yorktown during the siege?

What did the people who lived in America during the American Revolution go through and why should we remember them?

www.ingramcontent.com/pod-product-compliance
Lightning Source LLC
LaVergne TN
LVHW061257100826
845148LV00008B/1157
* 9 7 8 0 7 8 8 4 4 9 6 7 3 *